Why I Can't Be A Conservative

Mel C. Thompson

Copyright © 2023

Mel C. Thompson Publishing
3559 Mount Diablo Boulevard, #112
Lafayette, CA 94549

melcthompson@protonmail.com

Cover Photo Credits

Wikimedia Commons photo: "Texas Longhorn in the prairie grass, Wichita Mountains Wildlife Refuge, SW Oklahoma." Author: Larry Smith, August, 2014.

MCTP Book Design and MCTP Artists

For information about Mel C. Thompson's graphic design work for book covers or page design work for book interiors, or for any other inquiry regarding other MCTP artists and writers, please use the contact information above.

Table of Contents

What This Book Is And Isn't

This book probably won't be of much assistance to anyone's effort to rhetorically defeat conservatism or the GOP. While it's true that I've spent a lot of my life, if not most of it, attempting to convince others not to be politically, religiously or culturally conservative, this book is not a part of that effort. (To the extent that the book sometimes veers into being actively critical, it disproportionately targets all things DNC-related.) And so it's not likely anyone can use this book to help them make conservatives see the light and become DNC voters. There are books which attempt to aid in such efforts, but this book isn't one of them.

The purpose of this book is not to argue with conservatives or to give DNC voters any pointers on how to gain the moral high ground over conservatives. As far as this book goes, the bulk of it will consist of describing what conservatives believe and why I can't have those beliefs. And while I might have good conservatives friends, the contents of this book outlines why it would be impossible for me to vote with them.

This book exists to clear up a consistent point of confusions which, I admit, may be partly, or even largely, my fault. I have accidentally given some Democrats the impression that I'm conservative, and I've accidentally given some conservatives hope that I might be converting to their world-view, therefore it's incumbent on me to show, in explicit terms, why my belief system directly contradicts the core economic, political and religious beliefs of most conservatives.

One could think of this document this way: It's a policy platform which would immediately lead to my defeat were I ever to run in a GOP primary (and don't worry; readers right and left need not fear my ever running for office because such a spectacle would be sheer madness).

Like all full-time, progressive critics of the Democratic Party, I'm confronted with the question, on a regular basis, "Well, if you dislike the Democratic Party so much, why don't you just become a Republican? If you think the DNC, and everything associated with it, is so odious, why don't you just become a registered Republican and be done with it?"

Now such questions don't just come from Democrats, but also from conservatives of all stripes, including Republicans. "If you dislike the mainstream media so much, why don't you go 'the whole Dave Rubin' or do 'the whole Tim Pool?' If you're so miserable about woke media, why not just get away from all that and come on over and join us conservatives?" ("You know in your heart you want to," ect.)

At the heart of the matter is the fact that I won't be voting this year. But this is not for petty reasons, or due to undue pickiness or perfectionism, but simply because my particular belief system has ceased to have any official representation at the party level (and I have come to nickname my belief system something like "1990s liberalism," a form of liberalism which has been, at least at the public level, discarded at every major institution I've been involved in for the past third of a century). My very public refusal to vote for either Democrats or Republicans has made social and institutional life for me almost impossible. I am politically homeless; and not being willing to lie about what I believe has been the most expensive proposition of my life. In any case, at least in the Bay Area where I live, the ongoing presumption is that if you're not voting for Democrats, you certainly must have "secretly gone white nationalist."

In spite of this state of affairs, this book will only scratch the surface of what I would say were I to devote a whole book to the project of deconstructing the DNC. Even though I will certainly deliver scathing rants against the DNC in this text, still, discrediting the DNC is not my primary motive for creating this particular publication. Again, the goal of the book will be to continually remind the reader why I can't be a conservative. (Merely despising the DNC is not, contrary to popular opinion, enough to quality a person as a conservative, although I might agree with conservatives on this one point: Self ID is not enough. You have to actually be what you claim you are, politically, theologically and physically.) So it's not the primary purpose of this text to detail each talking point I might have against what conservatives call "the cathedral" or what the few remaining 1990s liberals call "the woke zombie apocalypse," although, no doubt, this work will repeatedly attack the particular type of DNC world that my own Bay Area has created (and still runs).

And while I might, at times, get polemical and rail at that globalist machine known as the DNC, there are now a few full-time critics who do a far better job than

I can of deconstructing and discrediting mainstream media, mainstream academia, mainstream tech and the identity-driven, DNC consensus-coalition. And so I refer the reader to them, as they are the true experts at lambasting the billionaires who claim to love us. I recommend that people explore such opinion-media figures as Russell Brand, Jimmy Dore, Matt Taibbi, Glen Greenwald, Max Blumenthal, Aaron Maté and Bill Maher (and here I even include people like Joe Rogan who would, were 1990s liberalism to return to the DNC, easily and happily retract their provisionally conservative posture). Also included would be such New Media alternatives as "Breaking Points" and "The Hill." Most of the people in this list of shows, with some exceptions, are natural-born liberals (some even Socialist and Marxist) who can explain, in all their YouTube splendor, how the DNC, and the arts, and tech, and the media (and almost every major institution in the western world) became fully authoritarian and thereby eradicated my style liberalism as a force in partisan politics.

So I'm not writing this book in a vain attempt to compete with or somehow surpass the work of the aforementioned commentators. And this book isn't primarily about attempting to win anyone over to any position (although I will sometimes give in to that temptation, especially at the end of the book). Here I will be attempting something much more mundane, to create a kind of inventory of my political positions (not so much to justify them, but to clearly list them).

In fact, I deliberately intend to present an incomplete defense of my policy positions (if I even defend them at all). The important thing for me here is to explain what my beliefs are and aren't. And because Democrats specifically proclaim that I ought to either vote for their candidates or join the conservative side, I will make it a point to keep coming back to the reasons why I can't join the conservative side. And while I will surely give in to the compulsive temptation to restate my long list of grievances against the DNC, still, I will attempt to remember that my goal here is to show why an RNC vote won't be happening for me. (My last ballot came in the mail and I promptly threw the whole thing in the trash.)

In this "binary choice" age, it's considered by most polemicists that no serious person could refuse to be conservative if they have a list of objections to the DNC that is a mile long. But I am confident that the reader, even a short way into this text, will see quite quickly why voting for most conservative policies can't possibly be in the cards for me. And once a person reads this tract and sees the position I'm in, they'll see that I would fail to become a real conservative even if such a thing were attempted.

Another way of thinking of this book is like an ideological address book. The location, so to speak, of people in my condition, who have beliefs largely attendant to such a condition, could hardly find a way to live in the conservative ideological neighborhood. Of course anything is possible. There might really be a conservative on earth who agrees with me; and so I say this to everyone: If you can find any person who claims to be a conservative and yet somehow has the same beliefs I do, I personally will go into debt to buy them all the drinks they want at their favorite bar. (So far, regarding that very public invitation, there have been no takers, further indicating to me that there just is no such beast.)

And now on to my actual beliefs, something that almost no one remembers, in spite of the fact that my beliefs haven't changed since 1988.

I'm Not A Religious Conservative

In attempting to discover whether someone is conservative or liberal, we find that we can never achieve 100% certainty, however we can estimate approximately how probable or improbable the case is. Therefore, no one single trait is decisive here, however, we can build up a kind of portfolio of traits that make it highly likely, or highly unlikely, that a person could be a conservative. The issue is not resolved with one paragraph, or one sentence, or the listing of any one feature or idea. But let's start with the biggest trait that we know of, and work onward from there.

While not every Evangelical Christian, or any other type of religious conservative (whether Mormon, Eastern Orthodox or Jewish Orthodox) is always politically conservative, it is, statistically, the leading indicator of conservatism among all other metrics. In my own case, as far as religious doctrine goes, I'm a flaming liberal. Hence, unlike religious conservatives, I don't hold any one sacred book to be the literal word of God. Hence, I don't believe that books like the New Testament, the Torah, the Quran, or any other such book, contains literal commandments actually written by God or by humans being directly commanded by God.

This refusal to be bound by any sacred book is not only the leading indicator of religious liberalism, but also the leading indicator of political liberalism. In short, one of the leading tests of whether a person is a political conservative is their willingness to believe that a book was written by God, or under the direct inspiration of God. Once anyone refuses to submit to the Bible, or any book claiming similar authority, the odds of them actually being politically conservative go down dramatically.

Now, I myself am leaning toward a kind of pantheistic polytheism in which no sacred books have much more than poetic authority (and poetic authority, while impressive, can't ever rise to the level of law-giving). This means I'm not monotheistic, not a believer in "the one God" of conservative Christianity, conservative Judaism or conservative Islam. Nor do I identify with any theology that is sexually conservative or highly restrictive regarding the intake of certain foods or beverages. As such, I am also theologically excluded from Orthodox Hinduism and Orthodox Buddhism. I have many gods and many lovers; and I eat red meat and drink red wine with enough gusto to fully alienate the average religious conservative. (If you didn't know Buddhism and Hinduism could really be politically conservative, you haven't studied Asian culture very much. And no, Buddhism and Hinduism aren't cool just because they're non-Christian. Everywhere and anywhere Hindus and Buddhists form a majority, the rules get really strict and really conservative, and quickly. Just like Evangelicals, believers in Asian religions are not really liberals either, even though they, like Muslims, remain in the Grand DNC Voting Coalition just to hide out from criticism.)

The Washington Post, in a story dated September 6, 2017, lays this out pretty clearly. The story, in fact, is entitled, "The stark racial and religious divide between Democrats and Republicans, in one chart." What we have in the story is actually two pie charts. The second pie chart shows the percent of Democrats who are white and Christian; and here we see the Democrats coming in at a smallish 29%. But the other pie chart shows that the percent of Republicans who identify as white and Christian being 73%.

Since I'm blatantly non-Christian, that alone starts us out at a 73% chance that I'm not conservative. This, in itself, is not conclusive, but it's a strong start, given that it's only one item among many that will be covered in this work.

Additionally, we must consider that, aside from mainline denominations, there are many conservative sects, churches and synagogues which are famous for their conservatism. The Mormon Church comes immediately to mind as they are overwhelmingly conservative. And besides them, there are Orthodox Jews. Because Orthodox Jews are a bit more private about making their political opinions public than Evangelical Christians are, I'm going to go here with an anecdotal piece of evidence.

Eric Metaxas, a "notorious" conservative Christian commentator and lifelong New Yorker, has had the opportunity to make private acquaintance with extremely religious Jews (and here I am not speaking of people who attend Reformed synagogues in Silicon Valley). What I'm referring to is traditional, religious Jews who believe in the Torah and all of the commandments in it (most of those commandments being extremely conservative in nature). Metaxas said in an online, live interview (which I personally watched) that the overwhelming majority of Orthodox Jews he knew were voting Republican.

Additionally, it must be noted that Orthodox Muslims (and here I don't mean the MFA girls walking around Berkeley living a completely secular life) are not really liberals at all. They are temporarily voting Democratic only because the Democratic Party, in exchange for their vote, has promised to shield Islam from all criticism by using their power over the media to label all critics of Islam as racists who can never again be allowed to work, or go to college, or participate in any major institution.

But the media-mafia's protection-from-criticism racket comes at a high price. In exchange for not having to have their feelings hurt by hearing criticism, most US Muslims agree to vote for a party that has virtually nothing in common with the truly Islamic lifestyle. In fact, right now, I spend every day studying Islamic Law, and I can't think of anything more antithetical to it than the beliefs of California coastal women. And so I issue this warning: Once the demographics of our country change to where the overwhelming part of the population is conservatively religious, then Evangelical Christianity, Orthodox Judaism and Orthodox Islam will team up to make sure this is an irreversibly conservative country. How do I know?

When we look at countries throughout Asia and Africa where the population is conservatively religious, but the mixture of religions includes Islam, we see instantly that Muslims band together with their rivals (the conservative Christians, Hindus and Buddhists) to ensure that most of what is called "the liberal agenda" never sees the light of day again. In Asia specifically, blasphemy laws are in force for multiple religions at once, meaning that secular people have to mind their manners quite strictly. In such situations where secular, humanities-oriented liberals are in the minority, Muslims instantly abandon any pretense of liberalism and cease voting for anything that looks like our Democratic Party. And, as I previously noted, they are quite able to join with Christians, Animists, Hindus and Buddhists to make sure that nothing like the lifestyle lived in San Francisco is permitted. True, these religions may be in competition for dominance, and may even be engaged in tit-for-tat violence, but, when it's time for the legislators who represent various groups to do their thing, they always agree to keep the social life of the country conservative and rarely opt to "celebrate our diversity."

Therefore, could Muslims vote in the US according to the actual teachings of their religion, as opposed to voting for protection from criticism, they would instantly be involved in some school of conservative political thought. They are not Socialists. Go to any Muslim marketplace and you'll see raging Capitalism and strict religious morality often come together. They are not, and never will be, Marxists from Manhattan. In that way, the 1% of the country that is Muslim (the percent that many elections are decided by) remains Democratic for now, but only for now. Could they speak their mind (and not offend The Grand Coalition of all parties fleeing criticism) they would sound a lot like conservative Christians, politically.

I mention all this to say that conservative Christians, Orthodox Jews, Orthodox Muslims and Orthodox Mormons are overwhelmingly conservative in their disposition and lifestyle; and, if they vote Democratic or speak as if they're liberal, they do so out of fear of losing their careers or because they're basking in the easy life that comes with never having to defend your ideas.

In any case, since I myself am not Christian, Jewish, Muslim or Mormon, the odds of me being conservative are already cut by at least 73%. As further evidence, I cite my own body of work, which is freely viewable to the whole world online and in print. Virtually a third of my work is religious comedy or the rewriting of religious mythology. To some I'm considered an outright blasphemer. and there are not many accused blasphemers who are secretly harboring right-wing fundamentalist values. Again, it's possible, but highly unlikely.

There just is no escaping the fact that the single largest component of the conservative movement is religious conservatism or religious traditionalism. And there's just nothing about me that smacks of conservative or traditional religiosity. I am religious, but an extremely liberal religious person, so much so that I get accused of outright Atheism or Agnosticism. There's just no part of my life or work that is edging or leaning towards anything like the beliefs held by your average Born-Again Christian from Arkansas. That just isn't happening.

I Believe In High Taxes

The reader may object, "But I know plenty of non-Christians who are conservative. Why does one get to claim to be a liberal by merely being non-Christian?" And here I would agree with that objection. The profile of the non-conservative needs to be filled out a bit more, and what better place to start than by describing what motivates most of the non-believers who remain in the conservative fold. And so let's go to the Atheist-conservative profile and it's main characteristic.

So you might know of a conservative who is not only irreligious, but overtly anti-religious. He's voting alongside fundamentalists of every sort, and yet he doesn't believe a word of the Bible and thinks 99% of the ideas issued from the pulpit are pure fairy tales at best and harmful mind-control at worst. So then how is it that he forms a coalition with religious people? What part of their Venn diagrams overlap. The answer is simple: Taxes!

While not every conservative Christian hates high taxes, most of them do. And while not every Atheist is conservative, the ones that hate high taxes are. And so here we find the basis for the conservative coalition. Furthermore, there are some Atheists who mock religion, but are not very upset by its presence in the world; and there are some Christians who deplore Atheism, but find that they rather like the personalities of anti-tax people of all stripes. If, by chance, any particular conservative Christian makes some allowances for a bit of sinful alcohol and tobacco consumption, and if privately they might like to tell naughty jokes, they might find their Atheist, anti-tax brother to be quite an amiable companion.

Furthermore, there are conservative Christians who like the honestly of the more offensive Atheists (now passed off as racists by The Guardian and Daily Beast crowd). Offensive Atheists are considered by Democrats to be a danger to The Grand Coalition because they freely attack Christianity, Judaism and Islam alike (and the rules of The Grand Coalition hold that Islam and Judaism may never be criticized because they are a part of The Grand Coalition and therefore may not be questioned). The rules of The Grand Coalition are explicit. Unless you want to be labeled as something akin to a white supremacist and excluded from society forever, you are to, forever, only attack Evangelicalism, Mormonism and Scientology (since none of those groups are useful to their coalition) and, as any bitter right-winger will remind us, Democrats simply discard and forget anyone not immediately useful to their latest collection of talking points. There is no loyalty in the Democratic Party, and there is no forgiveness and no redemption, making the whole enterprise, oddly, more morally bankrupt than the most sour of fundamentalisms since , in my experience, fundamentalists are at least loyal, do actually forgive and believe in redemption (something the scrunchy-faced, gray-haired, gray-backpacked, hunched-over Berkeleyites could barely conceive of as they lumber along Shattuck in something akin to a Thorazine haze).

But, returning to my mission here (and please excuse my rather impulsive diversions) I merely make the point that when we ask, "What on earth is an Atheist doing in the conservative coalition?" The answer is that they have found some overlapping beliefs and some overlapping mutual admiration. The Atheist may continually badger his fundamentalist friend for believing in "children's bedtime stories," but the fundamentalist takes this in good stride since he knows his Atheist conservative friend hates taxes and also serves as a good attack dog against theological rivals he himself might not have the courage to go after.

And here's a secret everyone has to pretend not to know: Many a fundamentalist secretly believes God will exempt the conservative Atheist from damnation for joining with him "to keep the rabble at bay." And too, the conservative Atheist, in addition to being rabidly anti-taxation (often sporting a "Taxation Is Theft" bumper sticker) like the fundamentalist, is a family man who insists on strict discipline, hard study and a full work week. Yes, he might be a chainsmoker who overdoes it with the gin-and-tonic, but, as the fundamentalist secretly sees it, God will make certain doctrinal exemptions for lives well-lived by anti-tax family men who lack proper theological insight. (And anyway, who else is the fundamentalist to go to when he himself needs a bit of weed and whiskey and soft-core porn?)

The Atheist, for his part, tolerates the silliness of certain Christians if those Christians are using the financial and political power of their church to protect his free speech as he lambastes not just Christianity, but all of the religions and sects Evangelicals take issue with. In fine, the offensive, anti-tax Atheist and the anti-tax Evangelical are fine political bedfellows, not the least reason for this being that, unlike people in The Grand Coalition, they can argue out and debate their differences. The Grand Coalition can't even admit that differences of ideology even exist, but rather they are relegated to a kind of good-person / bad-person standard, where all speech is content-free, aside from the regular denunciation of people as bad people who must be shunned versus good people who believe in basic human decency (and basic human decency will be redefined each week, since no word has any meaning for The Grand Coalition, aside from its temporary usefulness in terms of gaining the coalition more of the power it seeks; and again, we don't know what the coalition is, but we know that it must go on forever).

Over and against the conservative coalition, I'm overtly and proudly for substantial taxation. I'll never believe their mantra that taxation is theft. And while I regret the suffering involved in paying taxes, I don't see myself advocating for lower taxes for the foreseeable future. In fact, in certain cases, and in certain contexts, I might support substantially higher taxes than are now being paid by some sectors of society. In this way, I would be an awkward member of an anti-tax crowd because I would be maintaining that taxes are probably about where they need to be; and then I might even add some suggestions as to where taxes might be raised.

Again, my mission here is not convince anyone to actually believe in my positions on taxation, nor am I, for the purposes of this project, imploring the conservative reader to please advocate with me for the taxes he opposes. My mission is merely to show that the bulk of the conservative world consists of two types of people: conservative Christians who believe in low taxes and Atheists who believe in low taxes. Since I just don't believe in low taxes at all, it's hard to see myself fitting in with the Evangelical or Atheist side of conservatism, which doesn't leave much of conservatism for me to align with. The math just isn't there. In a crowd of Christian and Atheist anti-tax crusaders with families, houses, cars, wives, kids and pets, it's hard to see where a polytheistic, pro-tax renter with no houses, cars, spouses, kids or pets fits in. At this point then, the idea of me actually becoming a conservative borders on fantastical, and so I think, at this point, I have answered the often asked question, "If you dislike the Democrats so much, why don't you just become a Republican or Evangelical?"

But I am a person who likes to complete a project once it's begun. And so now that I have decided to answer this question which has been put to me countless times in countless ways, I figure I might as well just go all the way and explain most of the differences I have with conservatism. And additionally, it's important for me to answer more than one critic in the art world who, it has been reported to me, goes around whispering to people that I'm a secret right-winger. (And I would like to commend the brave people who came to me and told on those people, since The Grand Coalition has one rule that is usually inviolable, "Don't tell!" And so I must here amend my previous statement and say that apparently there are a few exceptions to my "Democrats have no loyalty rule." There are, it turns out, a few loyal Democrats in my life, though not many).

Now there are some who might argue that all of this seems overly defensive, but I take issue with that since I believe in self-defense. Since pop psychology took over our culture, there's been an automatic acceptance of the idea that anyone who defends themselves is either guilty as charged or some far-right madman. Good Democrats, it is taught, though not overtly (and I really had to corner people to get them to admit this) are never to defend themselves against any accusations The Grand Coalition levels at them. If they do so, and they are men, they are first to be ridiculed as failing to be good gentlemen. (True gentlemen, so goes the Democratic metrosexual teaching, are to — and I was told this in these words — "accept the abuse like real men.") Furthermore, self-defense is seen as heresy in the DNC media world where accusation equals guilt because that's what makes "our movement" powerful. Any successful self-defense, by definition, would prove The Grand Coalition to be wrong, and that could cause them a temporary loss of power, a prospect they simply lack the spiritual resources to cope with.

Again, self-defense must always be wrong because The Grand Coalition can never be wrong; and the coalition can never be wrong for two reasons: 1. They must never be seen to lose power, not even for a brief moment, and, 2. They can't be wrong since they have no beliefs and are prepared to forget anything they've said and erase anything or anyone at any moment to avoid even the most brief instant of embarrassment.

(One way of understanding all this is by referring to it as total spiritual bankruptcy.)

But here The Grand Coalition is fully misguided. All human beings, whether physically or verbally attacked, have an inherent right of self-defense. And it actually doesn't matter that their defense is defensive. In fact, now that I think of it, if defense isn't defensive, what would it be? How very odd that merely protecting ones self has been made out to be a kind of moral crime. Surely this trend in our culture is the result of nothing but psychological snake-oil and socially manipulative bullying.

I'm A Big Government Liberal

If you know any conservatives, go and ask them, "Would you consider yourself a pro-welfare, big-government type who's okay with high taxes?" If you think logically about it for a minute, you'll see that the person you questioned would think you were joking with them, because such a question directed at them couldn't even be serious.

If you're so locked into your bubble that you don't know any conservatives, Google: "conservative views on big government, high taxes and the welfare state." What will follow will be about ten thousand pages of seething invective by conservatives against high taxes, big government and the welfare state. This is not to say that all conservatives always want to cut all welfare and always eliminate all taxes, but rather to point out that the wider goal of conservatism, from a fiscal standpoint, is to have taxes be as low as possible, have the government be as small as possible and to reduce the welfare state as much as possible. True, some more sensible conservatives would rightly caution that one ought to approach all these projects with much circumspection and quite slowly so as not to create immediate social chaos. But this in no way changes their central world view, that it's possible (so they believe) to have a minimalist government, hardly any welfare and really low taxes, and still somehow maintain something like ordinary social order. My goal here is not so much to dispute these conservative beliefs, but merely to point out that I simply don't believe them.

Again, my goal here will not be to produce a vast refutation of small-government conservatism, but merely to show that I can't be a conservative because the central mood of conservatism just doesn't look like anything that goes on in my head. I, for one, believe in a truly massive welfare state, one bigger, by far, than our current one. (But I don't believe in state ownership of most enterprises, so I also reject State Socialism, hence I don't fit in with The Democratic Socialist Party of America or The Communist Party USA, nor with any such "people's" anything). I am, it must be repeated, a 1990s type of liberal: lots of government, but not all government; lots of taxes, but not total taxation; lots of welfare, but lots boundaries and accountability around that welfare. Again, my blend of beliefs, while shared with some small contingent of Americans, has no official party that celebrates that blend of beliefs; and so I remain politically homeless, as do millions of other people.

I don't fit in with the Democratic Party as the bulk of their energy is focused on calling people racist and sexist and homophobic. And while I agree that racism, sexism and homophobia exist, I don't believe in hunting people down, labeling them as such and then casting them out of society. (How very weird that the party that walks around with "Love Is Love" signs has, as it's central feature, vengeful, punitive mercilessness. And if you live in the Bay Area and have to see the ghoulish "in this house we believe" signs, you know how creepy these people are.) But again, however ugly the DNC mindset might be right now, there's no big-government, pro-tax, welfare-state guys in the GOP, and thus no way I can work for that team either.

This is not a matter of perfectionism or pickiness or prudishness. It's just that there's nothing like a real match there. The same goes for the Libertarian Party and virtually any other party that now has major visibility. There is some hope for The Forward Party, but any attempt at what I call true liberalism generally gets attacked and destroyed by the DNC or is totally taken over by the identity politics grifters and race-and-gender hustlers who no one knows how to say no to yet. In the end, my prediction is that The Forward Party, and all good-faith efforts at true liberalism, get painted as far-right and discredited in the mainstream media or get taken over by people who found out that, if no other career works, you can just call people racist for a living.

In any event, despite all of my cynicism and bitterness toward the DNC (and all of the intellectual diseases attendant to it) there's no hope of "taking revenge" by joining people who want to, as Steve Bannon routinely says, "dismantle the administrative state." After all, I'm all about the administrative state. I believe that regulatory agencies and welfare agencies must exist, and not just in a toothless, minimalist state, but in a serious, large and expensive state.

And here it needs to be said that just like 95% of all Socialists, Communists and Greens end up voting Democratic, 95% of all Libertarians end up voting Republican. So, in the end, The Libertarian party usually ends up, as a practical matter, just being a kind of distant extension of the Republican Party, just as the Greens, Communists and Democratic Socialists end up foot soldiers for the DNC. All that being said, I truly admit that those Socialists, Communists, Libertarians, and Greens who vote for their own party and don't vote for the DNC or GOP are "the real thing" and deserve some street cred for believing in something other than victory for victory's sake.

Still, I myself can't be a Socialist, Communist or Green because those parties don't merely believe in large government or high taxes, but more or less in the abolition of ordinary free enterprise. The extent to which they would tax, regulate, or even absorb businesses would essentially end Capitalism. And it's classic of 1990s liberals like me to believe in Capitalism, regulation, taxation and the welfare state as existing simultaneously. In that way, my ideology is just too inclusive for the narrow-minded world of today's DNC and GOP.

Capitalism is more robust than most Republicans think it is. I believe it can withstand substantial taxation and substantial regulation and not collapse. But the extent of regulation, taxation, or outright absorption of Capitalist businesses proposed by true Socialists, Communists and Greens is not even remotely acceptable to me (nor would it be to any 90s-centric liberal).

The word "Socialism" and the word "Fascism" are both now meaningless words in that the GOP and DNC have expanded their definitions to mean, "Shut up or I'll get you branded as a Communist or white supremacist." I assert that my definitions, which I intend to cover more fully in other publications, are pretty close to the real ones. The average American, completely under the sway of the GOP and DNC information networks, literally has no idea what most words even mean anymore, which makes political conversation almost impossible in my part of the country. In California, political conversation is literally impossible because most people here are just using race-and-gender language to deal with their post-traumatic stress and bipolar over-stimulation. This makes them not only anti-intellectual, but also boring and freakishly emotional. It would not be so painful to report that, except that a third of the people who used to be fun to talk to are now KPFA-NPR birdbrains who've had their intellectual curiosity trained out of them.

I Totally Support Gay Marriage

Back to those 70% to 80% of conservatives who are not only fiscally conservative but socially conservative (and religiously conservative). Well, since, at any given point, up to a third of my friends are either gay, bi or pan sexual, it's hard to imagine how on earth I could oppose gay marriage. In fact, I go to every gay wedding I'm invited to.

Now there are exceptions to every rule. And while it's true that most conservatives oppose gay marriage, it's also true that there are exceptions, Dick Cheney being one of them. But the overwhelming bulk of the conservative world is religiously conservative and opposes gay marriage on principle.

I, on the other hand, argued for gay marriage even when I lived in Orange County back in the days when it was infinitely more conservative and far less tolerant than it is now. And while support for gay marriage by itself is no indicator of liberalism, it's hard to even construct an idea of what a pro-gay-marriage, pro-big-government, pro-taxation, pro-regulation, pro-welfare, non-Christian conservative might be. Perhaps such a person exists somewhere, but I will literally pay $100 cash to the first person who can find a person who fits the above description and arranges for a meeting between me and that person. If such a person exists, I'd literally pay to meet them. (But if there is no such conservative with that list of beliefs, then I'm afraid it's impossible for me to be a conservative.)

I love Green Energy

There is no room in this pamphlet-length book for any kind of justification of green energy; and there is no attempt made here to launch a successful argument for green energy initiatives. In fact, I'm even okay if conservatives call me irrational and sentimental regarding such things. My purpose here is just to continue to show how different I am from the average conservative on so many issues; and green energy is one of them.

We can start, just for instance, with electric vehicles. My orientation is such that I always loved them, long before Tesla was even a thing. My fantasy, whether or not it was realistic, was to live to see a world full of electric cars powered by a power grid that was fed by solar panels and windmills. And there are now surfacing many compelling arguments that I can't go into here which cast a certain amount of legitimate doubt on my green vision.

All that being said, at every turn, and in every way, I was always, and still do, cheer on all efforts to create a world full of low-cost, sustainable electricity. At great expense to myself, I even turned off my natural gas for years and ran my whole home only on electric energy. (True, I lately was forced by this cold winter to install a new gas heater in order to survive, but I did this with great reluctance.)

But my whole orientation is one of attraction to a green electric world and a disinclination toward gas-powered things. From a very early age I was crippled by allergies; and one of the things I noticed really set my allergies off was gas fumes. Whether it was the "dirty," rumbling truck on idle that was pumping brownish smoke into the air, or whether it was the gas-powered lawn mower that smelled like a barbecue gone wrong or the gas-powered leaf-blower ruining my sleep at seven in the morning — I always disliked all of that.

Loud motorcycles waking us up at one in the morning, the smelly, exhaust-belching ferry-boat engines, the smell emerging from a restaurant-kitchen air-duct that hasn't been cleaned in years — all of it was always a turn off to me, and all of that always made my allergies worse.

But again, I make no attempt here to convince conservatives to repent and go green with me. In fact, I concede that much of "the science" may have been weak on these topics. And perhaps it's even possible that the mainstream media has been selective on green energy topics, perhaps only choosing to report stories that lent flattery to the cause while deliberately neglecting scientific findings that were unflattering to "the cause." Even so, my orientation is to still spend extra money I don't really have to support green causes (like my choosing to ride, just last night, a "green" ride-share vehicle to the train station).

Whether I'm right or wrong in terms of the viability, affordability or sustainability of green energy, my whole way of being has been such that I've been quite a fanboy for it, maybe even a dupe for it. The same cannot be said for the typical conservative.

I Love The California High-Speed Rail Project

California is a kind of worst-of-all-worlds for poor people and transportation. Other than San Francisco, most of it's cities are glorified, sprawling suburbs with laughably-small core districts. It's a world of pinchy-faced censors and white-shaming, finger-wagging feminists who, in spite of their sanctimonious self-righteousness, almost never do anything to get more housing or infrastructure built for the poor. (I would complain less if these mask-bearded, tattoo-laden soy-boys would actually put out to get low-income housing built along with awesome mass-transit facilities.) But alas, we must put up with conversation-impaired, Russia-collusion-believing, NPR-worshipping, KPFA-doting culture warriors who take ten years just to get an extra BART stop built.

But here I again must cite my own irrationality. I doggedly support California high-speed rail in spite of it being, at this point, a colossal failure; and I would be emotionally devastated if the project were ever abandoned. And yes, I understand the conservative harping about the insane and inexcusable cost-overruns regarding the project, but nonetheless, I can't give up the dream. Having been on high-speed trains in Europe more than once, I'm unable to throw in the towel on such a project here. I must hope that one day it won't take all day and night to get through the central valley to get back home to Southern California. I understand that the odds of me ever getting to see such a thing are remote, but still I hang on.

Conservatives of every stripe (and I've talked to many in the last few years) are universally skeptical, critical, or downright hostile to the California High Speed Rail Project. And I can't even defeat them in any argument on the topic. But the point remains that it's an odd duck of a conservative who would love this glorious white elephant of a project. And thus we can only conclude that this adds to the mounting evidence that, whether I'm right or wrong about this topic, I'm just not eligible to be seriously considered a conservative given where I currently stand on it.

For reference, an August, 2022 study by the US High Speed Rail Coalition shows 66% of Republicans opposing the California High Speed Rail project. If we take that previously-mentioned number of 73% of conservatives being something like Evangelical Christians and then think of how many non-Christian conservatives oppose most of the high-speed rail initiatives, we can see that a pro-high-speed-rail non-Christian would be nearly impossible to find among the ranks of conservatives. I'm sure they exist, but again, this issue, added to all of the other ones I've cited, makes the charge of secret conservatism against me highly improbable.

I Don't Even Own A Car

Being on disability and not owning a car, I'm continually on mass transit. And while I live in the Bay Area, it must be noted that this bluest of blue areas still manages to have a completely laughable bus system once you get outside of the BART coverage area. Even in Bay Area counties with rail other than BART, the service is minimalistic, penny-pinching and stingy beyond madness. Truly there are counties deep in the third world that have better transit than Contra Costa County where I must live.

And so one might, at first glance, say that I can't really "vote," per se on the mass transit issue, but rather that poverty forces my hand. However, one way to look at how much I dislike the car-centered, conservative world is by looking at this: Many poor people in my county, people who are in far more debt than me and who must forego way more luxuries than I do, opt to have a car against all odds. I've known people, and more than one, to sacrifice having an apartment in order to keep their car; and, wouldn't you know it, in spite of their poverty, these people tended to be more conservative than me. And, being more conservative, they just don't dig mass transit.

In contrast, the moment I could escape Orange County and get to an area that had at least one serious mass-transit train system, I did. I've changed my whole world more than once just to get near mass transit; and I've just never known a conservative to do that. How many disabled, low-income, green-energy-oriented, mass-transit conservatives do you know?

My Voting Pattern Is Anti-Conservative

Before I gave up voting altogether, it must be noted that for decades I just did not vote for conservatives, except for in extremely strange circumstances. I didn't vote for George Bush senior or for W., didn't vote for Mitt Romney, John McCain, Bob Dole or Donald Trump. (And once upon a time I actually worked as a cold-calling fund-raiser for the Democratic Central Committee of San Diego during the Dukakis campaign. And, in spite of my seemingly anti-feminist rhetoric, I mostly voted for Democratic women for Senate and House seats. On top of that, most of my doctors, lawyers and therapists have been Democratic women.) It's just hard imagining a conservative man who would live in such a way.

All of that being the case, the reason people assume I'm conservative is because of my failure to seethe with hatred toward conservatives, which, for them, is a kind of litmus test for emotional bonding. If you can't hate conservatives to the point of creating self-induced ulcers, you just must be a traitor to all things progressive. In fact, in the Bay Area, life doesn't revolve around doing anything for the poor, the uninsured, the homeless, the drug addicted or the mentally-ill. It all revolves around hating conservatives. Here, no one ever, ever brings up issues surrounding housing, poverty, mental illness or drug-addiction. They only talk about those issues if I bring them up.

Thus, I argue that I'm the true liberal in the Bay Area. I consider Bay Area people to be far closer to being conservative than me, since, after all, merely hating other people doesn't get anything progressive done. In fact, it eats up all the energy so that no time or energy is left to work on progressive causes. And I can't help but wonder if all these millionaires with Ukraine flags and Progress flags and BLM flags in their yard aren't really faking it. After all, it costs nothing, in terms of taxes or zoning or hard policy work, to simply call everyone who disagrees with you a racist misogynist.

And I consider it suspicious that they gladly give the tens of billions of dollars we're spending on Ukraine to our defense contractors first. As a kind of post-boomer, I am entitled, like an old man, to say, "in our day," people who voted to spend billions on weapons and do nothing for the poor were precisely called conservatives (as were people who doted over the FBI and the DOJ). If you ask me, all these NIMBYs around me are just a bunch of rednecks in CRT clothing.

I Support The Decriminalization of All Drugs

Here I would, if I were a politician (God help us) begin to lose not only the support of religious conservatives, but most of the Atheist conservatives too. I was against the drug war from the beginning and the mass incarceration that followed. There was never any doubt in my mind that the sale and use of marijuana should be legalized. And I never thought a person should be in prison for using any drug. I would probably agree that most drug dealers should be in jail, but only because virtually all of them are committing tax fraud and doing money laundering. But, supposing a drug dealer reported all his income and didn't launder any money or commit any violent crime or property crime? Then, I myself could not agree with imprisoning such a person.

In any case, I'm not meaning to go into a long debate about such things as heroin, opioids, crack, meth, etc., but am only here mentioning that people who always were for the legalization of both gay marriage and marijuana are not usually conservative, especially if they're also non-Christian and for the spreading around of lots of welfare. And since I'm pretty much "guilty" of all of the above, I would rather be at a loss as to how to describe such an agenda as conservative.

I Always Loved The Idea of Universal Health Care

If there is a hard-core, far-right extremist, white supremacist who is somehow in love with universal healthcare, please send me a link to an article about such a person. I've never heard of anyone like that, so if they exist, clearly such a person would have to be pointed out to me. The truth remains that the vast majority of believers in single-payer healthcare or Medicare-For-All, or Medicaid Expansion, or any such thing, are just flat out liberals. There's almost no other word to use to describe them. True, a conservative legislator, as part of a compromise deal in which his own state or district gets some pork out of the deal, might permit the expansion of government-funded healthcare to more people, but it's never anything a real conservative pined for.

To give the reader some personal context, quite apart from any ideological persuasion, I was born with many birth defects and genetic issues which I go into detail about in other books and about which my regular readers are by now sick of hearing about (no pun intended). And what attracted me to, and made me hope for, Universal Healthcare was that after I was no longer covered on my parents' insurance, but before I got onto Medicare, there was virtually no serious healthcare available to me as I spent decades working very low-paying jobs which carried the cheapest of stingy HMO plans, all of which served me horribly or outrightly denied me care I desperately needed.

There were other personal issues with the current healthcare system. Friends of mine died because there were virtually no drug rehabilitation facilities. In one case a friend addicted to heroin was asked to wait three years for his turn to get into a rehab facility. I watched mentally-ill friends go homeless without treatment and disappear into the night never to be seen again. These anecdotes are not designed to convince conservatives to believe in universal health care, but merely to explain my personal interest in the matter. Additionally, I needed advanced ear surgery but could not get it due to how stingy the HMO insurance was toward low-income workers at the time. I am now 50% deaf because my own HMO lied to me and said there were no surgical interventions possible for my inner-ear deformities. Later, after I got on Medicare, I found out from real doctors that this wasn't true. And so, to be clear, I'm not for, as the Democrats are, HMO coverage for all, nor am I for, as conservatives are, a free-market Darwinian healthcare service; but I'm for high-quality, Medicare service for all (and by that I don't mean the sleazy option now called Medicare Advantage, which is just another way to steer lifelong victims of HMOs back into HMOs once they finally get Medicare).

Again, while I might seem to be sermonizing, I'm actually just trying to show both conservatives and Democrats alike that it's just not possible that I could join their team. Why, would this theme need to be repeated so many times? The need for repetition here is simple. Democrats simply are incapable of accepting rejection gracefully and must proclaim that anyone that rejects them is secretly alt-right, far-right or worse. And, additionally, I'm detailing my situation to show conservatives that it's unlikely, given their distaste for intensive, high-quality, low-cost healthcare for the poor, that I could get excited about their small-government cause.

I understand that my situation might be, to some extent, unique; and therefore this work does not ask conservatives to adopt my positions. It's easy enough for them to argue that my case was an unusual one and that the people I associated with were not typical. And thus, they could argue, there is no need to reconfigure a national healthcare system in order to help rare and unusual cases. I'm not saying I'd agree with their assertions, but merely that I could understand how they could arrive at their conclusions.

But, in all of these deliberations, one thing remains clear, I'm in favor of (even if for purely emotional and sentimental reasons) massive government intervention for the uninsured, the underinsured and those trapped in unresponsive HMO insurance plans. And conservatives, in general, with rare exceptions, are generally not happy to even contemplate the massive scale of medical rescue, dental rescue, rehabilitation rescue and mental health rescue that I'm hoping will one day happen. In conclusion, while conservative views on healthcare might have some validity, or may even prove to be superior to my views, I'll never be in a position to see that because the anecdotal evidence in my life, and in the lives of people around me, is too strong for me to overcome purely on intellectual grounds. Hence, I'm not even eligible to be conservative. Were I even, in a strictly academic way, to assent to small-government solutions to massive, national healthcare problems, that intellectualism would not be enough to carry the day against the sheer weight of personal disasters I had with the conservative, minimalist approach to healthcare I was exposed to for decades.

I Believe In Luck More Than Hard Work

Note that the title to this segment has the word "more" in it. I am not saying that I have no belief in the value of hard work. I do. However, the question here is not whether hard work is helpful or virtuous. The question is which plays a larger role in life. And on this issue there's just no getting around my incompatibility with the conservative outlook.

I was born with a set of physical and psychological problems in an environment ill-suited to the alleviation of certain aspects of those problems. At no point in my life was I not held back, derailed or stopped in my tracks by recurring health problems. Hard work helped me survive. Hard work prevented bad situations from getting even worse. Hard work was valuable, but I could never have the overall belief that the majority of conservatives have which is that life is what you make it.

There is an old conservative saying bandied about in motivational circles: "Life is 10% inspiration and 90% perspiration." The message could not be clearer: Luck, according to most conservatives, is a minor factor in determining whether or not a person will be poor or rich, successful or unsuccessful. And thus financially unsuccessful people are viewed in the conservative world with much suspicion and, in general, are presumed guilty of laziness and asked to please not offer any excuses for their condition but only to report back later after more hard work has resolved the matter.

Having grown up in a conservative environment, I can say with certainty that the very first instinct conservatives had was to reject out-of-hand anyone's claim to chronic illness unless they literally had more than two limbs cut off and were simultaneously blind and had an oxygen tank strapped to their wheelchair. Anything less dramatic than that was greeted with utter and total skepticism and humiliating accusations of malingering.

Even so, what I have just reported was not written as an attempt to get conservatives to believe me, but rather to show both conservatives and Democrats the social issues that would be involved with me trying to declare myself conservative. After all, I have been to conservative house parties, and the awkwardness is still palatable. "What do you do for a living? How much do you make? What's the problem? Why can't you make more? Couldn't you work harder? Can't you try harder? Can't you do more?"

Chronically ill people who can walk normally and talk coherently are simply not welcome in the conservative world unless they can report back to that world that they have conquered their economic problems. Oh sure, it's understood that one might go through a rough patch here and there (with the understanding that no rough patch may ever last more than a few months) but long-term economic failure can rarely be tolerated. Now of course there are exceptions, and indeed more than one conservative has ended up being very charitable regarding my situation; and for that I'm extremely grateful. But, by and large, in the county I live in, you can't even get into a conservative event without spending a hundred dollars in-advance and another hundred once you get in; and these events are held in places where a person arriving on foot (even if they could save the hundred dollars to get in) would look freakish. (A conservative who can't afford a car? You can't imagine how badly such a thing would come off.) And thus, to even meet with most conservatives to attempt to make friends with them would involve firstly getting my career to fly at several times the altitude that it does, and then it would involve me being able to maintain a car, and then after that there would still be the up-front costs of the meetings themselves. And thus, had I even wanted to be conservative, had I "seen the light" and converted to the conservative cause, one hardly knows which door a person in my condition could even enter into it by.

I Believe In Death-With-Dignity Legislation

Let us, to use Jen Psaki's term "circle back" to those religious conservatives. Not only are they usually opposed to all abortion, but also specifically opposed to right-to-die legislation. The purpose of bringing this up is not to argue against the religious views of conservatives (as it was originally-and-mostly religious conservatives who opposed death-with-dignity laws) but merely to point out that most conservatives are generally opposed, on moral grounds, to the right of terminally-ill patients to end their suffering through medically-assisted suicide. The reason this is key to my central thesis is that religious conservatives have won the day inside GOP circles to the point where they're even getting Atheist conservatives to be against medically-assisted suicide for terminally-ill patients. And this all shows, again, how I get further and further, every day, from being able to be categorized as a conservative

As a person who has had dozens of surgeries and countless painful medical procedures, I learned early on that most people have no idea what kind of pain is involved in chronic physical illness. The conservatives I grew up around were, on the whole, far physically stronger and healthier than me and suffered far less from debilitating depression or anxiety than your typically-progressive artistic type. And thus, not only were they morally opposed to right-to-die laws, but felt that the chronically-ill and chronically-depressed should just tough it out no matter what kind of pain came their way. And, I might add, virtually no conservative that I grew up around even believed chronic pain was real. We were continually told that people with arthritis were "faking it just to get attention" and that even some people walking around with crutches were just "trying to get sympathy."

Thus, the conservative world I saw as a youth would permit no such dodging of pain as might be afforded by death-with-dignity legislation. And even if the occasionally sympathetic conservative actually believed intolerable pain could exist, they still stuck to their moral objections to anyone ending their lives prematurely for any reason. But I, from the very start, disagreed with them and my position in favor of medically-assisted suicide has not changed even slightly in decades.

I Support The Legalization of Sex Work

In the artistic world, especially in the lower rungs of it where I tended to live, many people, even some men, had no option but to turn to sex work unless they wanted to go through the even worse humiliations that welfare recipients are put through. While I wouldn't wish a life of financially-compelled sex-work on anyone, I cannot bring myself to prohibit it if the sex worker feels they really have no other option for survival.

As a poor person myself who has had to, for many reasons, live in some of the most expensive cities in the world, I can testify that survival in the Bay Area (while being non-wealthy) is almost impossible; and the struggle to do so only added to my preexisting health problems and ultimately this resulted in incurable sleep disorders that has seen me going on and off disability and on and off various other unpleasant social programs.

But there's an even more unpleasant and unpalatable angle for me to discuss here. My appearance, along with my financial and social situation, is very unstable, hence "my story" seems inconsistent or even contradictory. I cannot resolve for the reader in the short space allowed in this document, all of the reasons why at one moment I could be propelled to nearly the top of the social ladder and the next thrown down literally into the gutter to socialize with homeless people, but suffice it to say, I really know what social desperation is.

And so I not only believe sex work should be legalized for people who feel they cannot earn a sufficient living any other way, but also it should be legal due to the sheer number of outcast men who feel they can't get physical attention any other way. In short, sex work is humiliating both for the worker and the customer, but I'm afraid I believe it's a necessary evil, so to speak. There just are too many desperate women and men who are unable to find their way into healthy and prosperous situations in which true love is even possible. I cannot, as religious conservatives do, simply order them to live more austerely and to resist to-the-end all such temptations.

Still, it's important to note that I'm not trying to present a deeply convincing and thorough argument in order to win conservatives over to my belief in legalized sex work. (I might embark on such an effort one day, but today is not to be that day.) But what I am seeking to do is to add legalized sex work to the long list of things I would legalize that typical conservatives wouldn't. True, any given conservative might be for legalizing one or two of some of the things I would legalize, but not all of them. And so my entry of sex work into this short catalog serves the purpose of showing how deep and far my liberal instincts go. I simply go too many places where conservatives dare not tread to be taken seriously as a conservative.

I Don't Believe In Patriarchy Or Ethnostates

Here, in the year 2023, I personally do not have any conservative acquaintances who actually believe that women should be excluded from certain roles in society or that people of color should be denied any opportunities based merely on their race. However, there are some famous conservatives who do and even a few who believe in a government based on racial, sexual or gender hierarchies. Democrats, for their part, hold aloft these examples and promote awareness of them 24/7 to the exclusion of all else. The DNC world emphasizes quotes and video clips of the few conservatives who really do believe in patriarchal ethnostates in order to sell the DNC's dishonest idea that most conservatives "secretly hope for a return to when men and whites ran everything." And because Democrats believe this (or rather pretend to believe it) all of us progressives who disagree with the DNC are humiliatingly forced to dilute the power of our own messages in order to announce the obvious, that we never believed in patriarchy or ethnostates. (DNC hacks have almost certain knowledge that most people are not racist, but they love forcing them to spend all their political energy proving they're not. They are absolutely addicted to the power this gives them and can never let that power go.)

The DNC has successfully forced everyone who disagrees with them to spend most of their time clarifying what they are not. (This makes dissent from within the progressive sphere virtually impossible most of the time.) This means only DNC hacks get to spend most of their energy forwarding their own agenda instead of having to refute false accusations.

The DNC loves this: While they're keeping you busy 24/7 trying to prove that the absurd allegations against you aren't true, they get to use all their energy to seize control of more charities, schools, libraries, entertainment venues, universities, publishing houses, medical institutions and corporations. This is the very power the DNC has used to force every major institution in the western world to submit to being used as the personal police force of the DNC. And they so love this advantage over everyone that they will never give it up no matter how many people it hurts; and they truly could never care about how many people they're hurting. This I found out from personal experience.

By the way, you will never, ever hear mainstream media use the word "ethnostate" because it's too specific and it's meaning can't be fudged. They instead use the phrase "white nationalism" because that phrase is so easy to manipulate and it's meaning can be changed daily or hourly. That kind of creepy manipulativeness is why I'll never vote for Democrats again.

In any case, since the Democrats have successfully sold half the country on the fraudulent idea that most conservatives are secretly racist and sexist and homophobic, it must be admitted that such bigotry is now associated with conservatism in people's minds. Thus, anyone doing a full exposition on why they're not conservative, must include a kind of North Korean struggle-session proclamation that, "We swear we aren't racist like the conservatives are," although most conservatives aren't even racist and Democrats already know that. The sadism of the DNC is unspeakable because they've put gatekeepers at the door of every institution to force this weird kind of language out of us; and they do it knowing that it's unnecessary (and, because they are sadists, the fact that it's unnecessary gives them an extra thrill).

In any case, as a garden-variety 1990's liberal, I simply never believed that things like housing, education, medical care, banking services, transportation, or public services of any kind, should be based on race, gender, sexuality or religion (or political beliefs). Democrats are training the world to believe that any disagreement with the DNC can only come from people who are white nationalists or people who are seeking an ethnostate. To the extent that any conservatives ever did propose such a thing, I always disagreed with it and never felt attracted to such ideas. I don't believe most conservatives are fighting for an ethnostate, but if they were, I surely would have even less interest in their doctrines.

I Don't Believe In Creationism Or A Flat Earth

Another way in which I differ from some religious conservatives, but not most of the Agnostic or Atheist conservatives, is that I don't believe in creationism, flat-earth doctrines nor any of the supernatural events described in the Bible, the Torah or the Quran. Certainly many conservatives, if they are conservative for strictly economic reasons, share my disbelief in such things.

While I'm not currently a paid scientist, I've had a bit of scientific study and involvement to mention. My degree is in Philosophy, but the department I went to valued Philosophy of Science very highly (along with math, which almost all experimental science is based on). Thus, even after leaving school, I have studied multiple levels of calculus, trigonometry, algebra, differential equations, geometry, statistics and linear algebra. On top of that, I've made an intensive study of scientific testing methods. Some philosophers, even amateur ones, can take the matter of scientific methodology very seriously.

The casual reader may not know that much of the structure of math and science was not invented by guys who worked at jobs as paid scientists. In fact, much of the structure of the mathematical and scientific world around them was the product of philosophers. Pythagoras, Aristotle, Descartes and Leibniz are prime examples. The very systems of reasoning that validated and promulgated science were indelibly intertwined with Philosophy.

The philosopher Descartes invented the Cartesian Coordinates you used in your early Algebra classes. The philosopher Pythagoras happened to invent the most foundational theory in Trigonometry. The philosopher Leibniz was one of the pioneers of Calculus itself. And much of the infrastructure of scientific investigation was set in motion by the exhaustive works of Aristotle.

Sometimes, when people with jobs in science (too often compromised by the interests of their employers and academic peers) can't get their lab to produce anything but junk science, philosophers have to be brought in, not because those philosophers know more about the exact scientific disciplines going on in those labs than the working scientists do, but because the scientists being paid to run those labs are inundated with political, financial and doctrinal bullying to the point where they can't even trust themselves.

The reason I mention all this is not to praise myself as some high-end scientist, but to merely show that science isn't foreign to me at all. But why would I go to the trouble to make such a point? Because the DNC media has trained you to believe that anyone who questions, criticizes or challenges their assertions only does so because they are far-right, ignorant, anti-science extremists. And this strategy has been wildly successful. You have to be in the Bay Area to see the sheer volume of humanities-graduates in the arts who, although they never got past Algebra II, believe themselves to be "only following the experts in science," because, you know, "they *are* the science."

Because I immediately saw all the really awful "science" going on in the realm of COVID mandates, and because I dared to disagree with things I knew to be patently superstitious, ideas that only peer pressure raised to the fervor of a religious purge could produce, I was branded as far-right and anti-science. Weirdly, it was not only humanities majors who did this, but specifically college-drop-out humanities majors (which made the whole spectacle even stranger).

I say all of this to point out that I am most definitely a liberal, most definitely pro-science and absolutely not an anti-science conservative (which I can't be anyway since I'm not a conservative at all). Again, in spite of these digressions, the point of the book is to show that most of the people the media is accusing of either being conservative or anti-science simply aren't.

The "experts" on NPR that Bay Area people listen to were not interviewed by scientists but by people with journalism degrees. (And I know because I went and checked their degrees.) And so I assert that they, the Bay Area DNC voters, are as likely to be ignorant about science as the people they are accusing of being anti-scientific; and, furthermore, I asset they don't even know the math to prove or disprove any numbers they're reading to themselves.

The fact that I point this out to them does not make me conservative. If anything, it's they who are conservative, since their beliefs are the product of conformist peer pressure and not their own scientific investigations. And the very hallmark of the old-world conservatism is precisely the kinds of closed-off minds DNC voters now have. Cancel culture, which they claim to disavow but actually get off on, is none other than just a new Salem witch trial, a new McCarthy hearing, nothing more than a mass-movement based on instant credulity. And that's not liberal at all. So they know nothing about science, nothing about the law, and nothing about true individuality. How is that liberal? They just agree with institutions that are controlled by billionaires? And since when was obsequious fawning over billionaire media some kind of act of "resistance?"

Now, the reason I can't be a conservative is exactly this: Whether the conservative, anti-science nightmare comes from the DNC or the GOP, or any other group in between, I will oppose it. That's what liberals do, and I'm a liberal.

You can see the DNC mind churching now: "Surely he's an anti-vaxxer!" But no. I have had all five COVID vaccines, as well as multiple flu vaccines, as well as shingles vaccines and tetanus vaccines (and the list goes on and on). I've probably had more vaccines than you have. But you'll see that you, as a DNC believer, if you've even made it this far, are casting about in your mind, trying to find a way to pin the conservative label on me. But here's a question: Why do you need to do that? Who trained you to do that? And how is it that a person as reflexively conformist as yourself considers yourself liberal? What's even liberal about you?

Become A Real Liberal

Now it may seem that I'm simply blaming the DNC for destroying the world as I knew it. Well, the reason it seems that way is because I am precisely blaming the DNC for exactly that. Be that as it may, there is no ideological home for me in the conservative world, as the bulk of the foregoing has shown.

I shall restate that my beliefs simply haven't changed since 1988. It is the DNC demand that I accept new beliefs that aren't liberal that caused me to leave the DNC realm. Even so, no amount of evil committed by the DNC and their media-tech-academia allies can ever make me conservative. In fact, it's the conservatism at the heart of the current DNC that has driven me away from it. It's an authoritarian hellhole from top to bottom. It's not conservative for me to want to get away from the race-and-gender baiting nightmare that is the DNC. In fact, most of the people I look up to as true liberals are people who've fled the DNC because they were people of conscience. (If you believe what most billionaires like Bill Gates, Tim Cook and Mark Zuckerberg believe, you can't be a conscientious objector. You have all the world's power behind you, and there's zero bravery in that.)

So my invitation to the reader is not to become a conservative just because the DNC has become an ethical monstrosity, but rather I invite the reader to join me in becoming a really real liberal, a person who questions first before agreeing, a person who deals in ideas rather than movements, a person who doesn't shut conversation down but opens them up, a person who talks to friends and enemies alike, a person who lets his or her ideas be tested in the crucible of cross-examination.

If you're afraid of what your enemies have to say, it could be argued, it's only because you suspect that what they're saying is true and you don't want to know. But this sort of cowardice is beneath us. And it's time you gave up your closed Facebook group where you all agree, in-advance, what the party-line will be. (And yes, my friends are in those groups and report back to me what you really say in there, which is grounds enough for me to never talk to you again, by the way.) Until you're free of all such groups, you can never reclaim your heritage as a free thinker. Yes, I know that you had no movement to belong to before then, but it's time you grew up and shed your need for movement-oriented validation. You need to learn how to actually have a real conversation again before you get so boring that your few remaining friends dump you for becoming such a dullard.

We should dump antiracism (which is just new racism) and antifascism (which is just new fascism) and invest all that energy into materially helping people of color and marginalized people, not with pronouns and pride celebrations, but rather with housing and medical care and real mass transit. So why won't you get behind that? Because it's you who aren't a real liberal, not me. You're just playing with words and focusing on hurt feelings. In your daily life, you put no energy, not even verbal energy, into tackling hard problems. Calling people racist is free, easy and requires no discipline or learning. And that's why you like it, because you're not only not really a liberal, but you're lazy and completely lacking in curiosity and imagination. And that's why I no longer like your people or vote for them. They're phonies and frauds to the core.

This all has led to an awkward thing, which is that, on a one-on-one basis, I've managed, against all odds, to secure a few conservative conversational partners. But why would I talk to people who disagree with me 75% of the time? Easy, they actually know how to have conversations, not conversations in which we agree all the time, but conversations in which ideas are freely bandied about, in which thought experiments can easily take place. When I talk to Bay Area Democrats, it's like swimming through molasses. It takes hours and hours just to get through the clarifications of what I'm not saying to ever get to what I am saying.

Communication itself with Democrats is all but ruined; and so I find myself, against all odds, when I have a choice, opting to try to get conservative conversation partners. True, as I previously said, many dislike me at the outset for all of the reasons listed in this book; and some really are narrow-minded and reject me out of hand for either my poverty or my blasphemous sense of humor. (Conservatives can be politically correct in their own way sometimes.) But, in spite of all these issues, I continue to try because when I do "score" a conservative conversation, the conversation is brisk, open, lively, fun and uncensored in contrast to the uptight, square, censorious, manipulative, passive-aggressive hostility and just plain narrowness of Bay Area people in general.

Therefore, although it's nearly impossible for me to fit into, in any broad sense, the conservative community, I must continue to seek out the quirky conservatives who, perhaps only privately, would engage me in conversation. Given that my theology is completely left wing (in terms of me not embracing any scripture nor any puritanical rules whatsoever) it's unthinkable that I could join a conservative church. And it goes without saying that I can't engage in conservative activism because it would be insane to actively work to get my own Social Security and Medicare cut.

But I need to talk. And the number of phobias around conversation that the average California Democrat has is becoming mind-blowing. And the number of required beliefs for membership in human society for them expands daily. The sheer amount of conformity and obsequious reverence demanded is just too prohibitive. They simply are no fun; and the once-lively art that Los Angeles and San Francisco produced is now so boring and lifeless and fake that I can hardly tolerate it.

And so this is true political and social homelessness. My own people are closed off to me, not because they even try to be closed off, but because they have shut themselves down and lack intellectual curiosity. However, "the other side" has many issues with me too, and so doing much intellectual work among them is unlikely at this moment in time. Therefore my political homelessness is not just a posture. It's the real thing.

Preface As An Afterword

In the fiefdom-like worlds of education, media, politics, employment, entertainment and sports, any true liberal who refuses to accept the new race-and-gender authoritarianism that has taken over 99% of our institutions, is immediately branded as an evil conservative. Most people are so thrown off by this, that they are bullied into silent compliance or they even join in with the creepy, woke racializing, genderizing and medicalizing of every issue (if for no other reason than vocational and social survival).

And with the intentionally-divisive good-person / bad-person dichotomy that is handed down by the woke media on every issue, the sincere and earnest liberal is left to scramble to even keep up with the new rules (all of them mandatory) and new terminology (all of it mandatory) required to even maintain their jobs and their friendships. In the rush of trying not to get crushed by this revolutionary power-grab, the honest liberal would hardly know were to begin to define what a real liberal or real conservative is.

Furthermore, if the unthinkable happens, and a liberal dissents on any woke issue whatsoever (whether that be Russia Collusion, MeToo, BLM, COVID or the Ukraine) they are then hopelessly, permanently and irredeemably branded as a conservative for whom there can be no forgiveness, fellowship or mercy. This situation is, by the way, the true essence of arch conservatism. (And how the Democratic Party became infinitely more conservative than the Republican Party will have to be a topic for another book.) But still the question comes: What do I say and what do I do if I'm accused of being a conservative when I'm an ordinary liberal?

We've all been trained by insidious one-liners not to defend ourselves against false accusations. The famous one-liners that come from our odious universities are: "Just because you have a black friend doesn't prove you're not a racist," or, "Just because you're poor and disabled doesn't prove you don't have white privilege," or, "Just because you're homeless and hooked on drugs doesn't mean you're not a misogynist." These sayings were developed in the universities to silence anyone who denies that they are racist, sexist or conservative. We've all been convinced that defending ourselves is "defensiveness" which allegedly has as its object "holding onto your power" because your "white fragility" causes you to be "afraid to give up your power."

What we have here is an authoritarian faction that isn't liberal or democratic. It's a bourgeois, oligarchic, decentralized dictatorship which has trained us not only to obey them by censoring everything we say, but by getting us to censor our own, natural urge toward self-defense. Well, I'm here to say that all true liberals should do, at a minimum, these two things in protest: 1. Never vote for Democrats again until DNC officials themselves condemn all of the racial, sexual, medical and military authoritarianism that has taken over our corporations, universities, financial institutions and media outlets, and, 2. At every turn defend our liberal credentials and assert that real aid to the poor and marginalized, in the form of housing, medical care, tuition assistance, psychiatric care, substance-abuse care and real mass transit, are the way forward for the true liberal party.

And, I assert, every true liberal who believes in real equality — not the sexist, racist identity politics that dominates college admissions offices and human resources departments — must insist that investments in upward class mobility will elevate people of all identities far faster than dehumanizing straight, white, downwardly-mobile, low-income males. The DNC needs to stop speaking truth to powerlessness and instead have the courage to break the corporate shackles that bind it to every bad idea on the planet.

While it's pretty self evident how to take care of the first item on my agenda. The second is tricky because everyone's forgotten how to do it. And so I've created this short tract to remind people what our main goals traditionally were and what they really should be now. And I did all this to encourage people to embrace everything that's truly and honestly liberal.

The people most attracted to the illiberal cult of race-and-gender politics have proven to be the very worst kind of friends in the private sphere and the most unimaginative and talentless artists in the public sphere. Intellectually and spiritually, they are simply bankrupt and boring. No greater collection of insufferably sanctimonious and cringeworthy phonies has ever existed. We must take our institutions and political processes back from them.

In the meantime, let this book serve as your first political self-defense manual; and I can only hope that others will come forth with better, more complete works on this subject. Again, since, the DNC has become everything it used to despise, we cannot, in good conscience, support it, and we must withhold our votes from it. (If we keep rewarding them with our votes, what motivation do they have to listen to us?) If they want our votes, they'll have to court us; and that will involve them working to bring free speech back to the public square, and the full restoration of human rights to people of all races (including whites and Asians) and all genders and sexualities (including men and straight people) and all religions and political beliefs (including conservatives and Christians). We, as true liberals must demand an end to the ideological segregation of society that woke Democrats have created. Ideological Jim Crow must go. But that journey of a thousand miles must start with one step: We must learn to defend ourselves; and this book is a true-liberal's self-defense manual.